DID DINOSAURS EAT PIZZA?

MYSTERIES SCIENCE HASN'T SOLVED

LENNY HORT

ILLUSTRATED BY JOHN O'BRIEN

HENRY HOLT AND COMPANY

NEW YORK

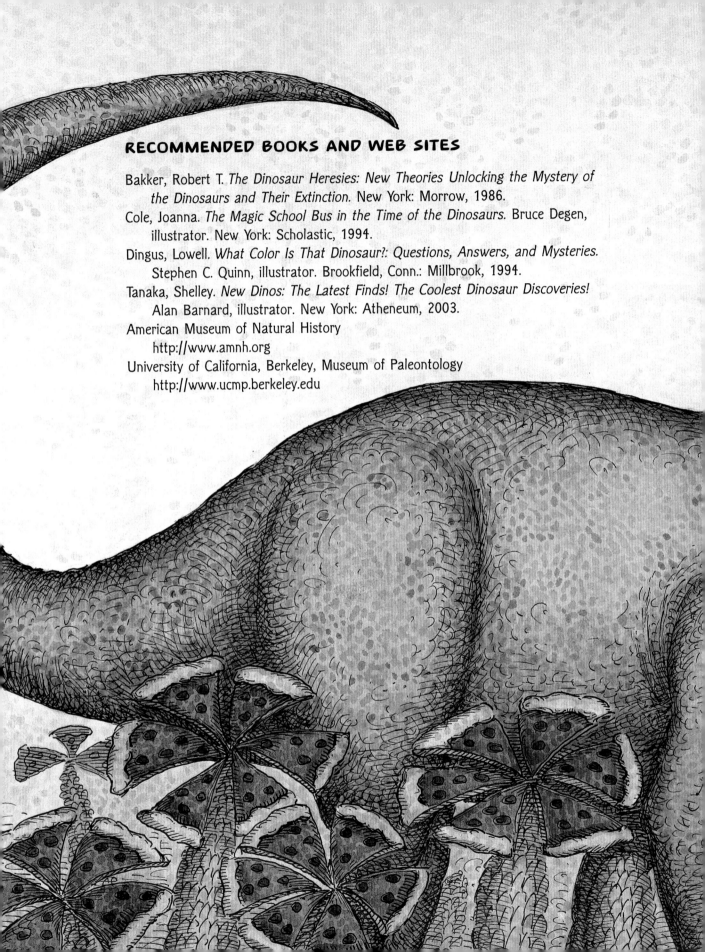

RECOMMENDED BOOKS AND WEB SITES

Bakker, Robert T. *The Dinosaur Heresies: New Theories Unlocking the Mystery of the Dinosaurs and Their Extinction.* New York: Morrow, 1986.

Cole, Joanna. *The Magic School Bus in the Time of the Dinosaurs.* Bruce Degen, illustrator. New York: Scholastic, 1994.

Dingus, Lowell. *What Color Is That Dinosaur?: Questions, Answers, and Mysteries.* Stephen C. Quinn, illustrator. Brookfield, Conn.: Millbrook, 1994.

Tanaka, Shelley. *New Dinos: The Latest Finds! The Coolest Dinosaur Discoveries!* Alan Barnard, illustrator. New York: Atheneum, 2003.

American Museum of Natural History
http://www.amnh.org

University of California, Berkeley, Museum of Paleontology
http://www.ucmp.berkeley.edu

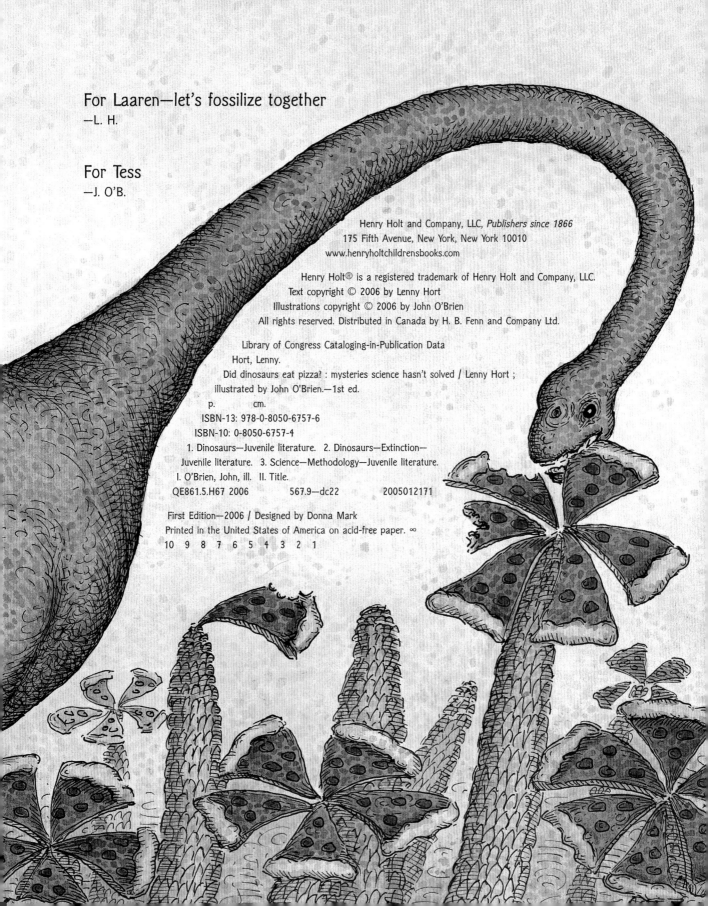

For Laaren—let's fossilize together
—L. H.

For Tess
—J. O'B.

Henry Holt and Company, LLC, *Publishers since 1866*
175 Fifth Avenue, New York, New York 10010
www.henryholtchildrensbooks.com

Henry Holt® is a registered trademark of Henry Holt and Company, LLC.
Text copyright © 2006 by Lenny Hort
Illustrations copyright © 2006 by John O'Brien
All rights reserved. Distributed in Canada by H. B. Fenn and Company Ltd.

Library of Congress Cataloging-in-Publication Data
Hort, Lenny.
Did dinosaurs eat pizza? : mysteries science hasn't solved / Lenny Hort ;
illustrated by John O'Brien.—1st ed.
p.   cm.
ISBN-13: 978-0-8050-6757-6
ISBN-10: 0-8050-6757-4
1. Dinosaurs—Juvenile literature.   2. Dinosaurs—Extinction—
Juvenile literature.   3. Science—Methodology—Juvenile literature.
I. O'Brien, John, ill. II. Title.
QE861.5.H67 2006   567.9—dc22   2005012171

First Edition—2006 / Designed by Donna Mark
Printed in the United States of America on acid-free paper. ∞
10 9 8 7 6 5 4 3 2 1

We know tons about dinosaurs, even though the last one died millions of years before the first human was born. But there's a lot we still don't know.

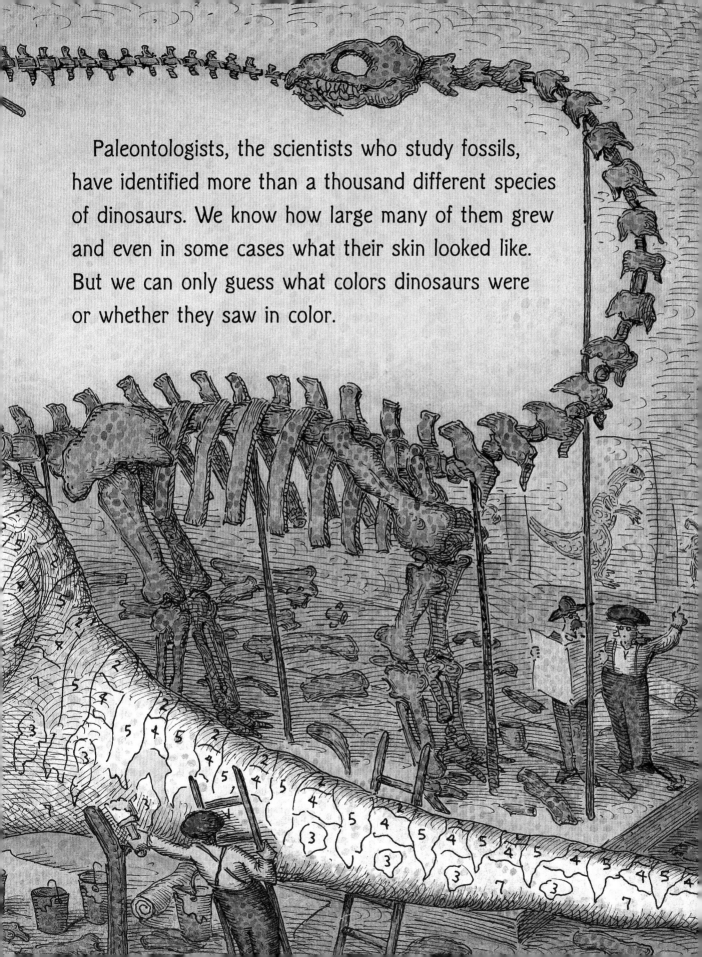

Paleontologists, the scientists who study fossils, have identified more than a thousand different species of dinosaurs. We know how large many of them grew and even in some cases what their skin looked like. But we can only guess what colors dinosaurs were or whether they saw in color.

We know from fossil teeth that most dinosaurs ate plants. But we don't know how such giant sauropods as Argentinosaurus or Seismosaurus

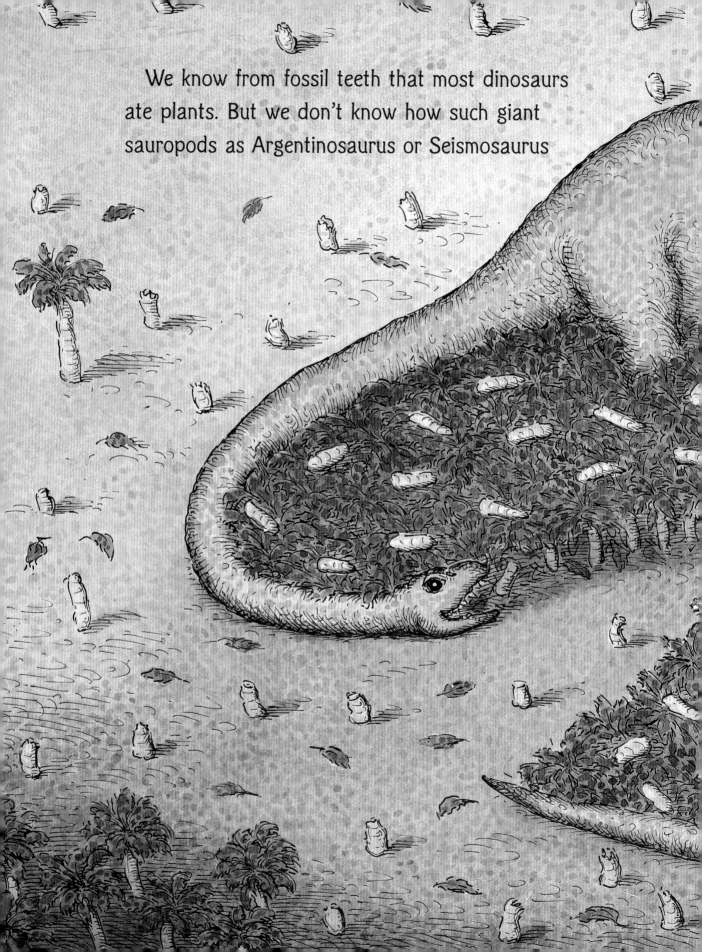

could ever eat enough to maintain a
weight that might have been as much
as one hundred tons.

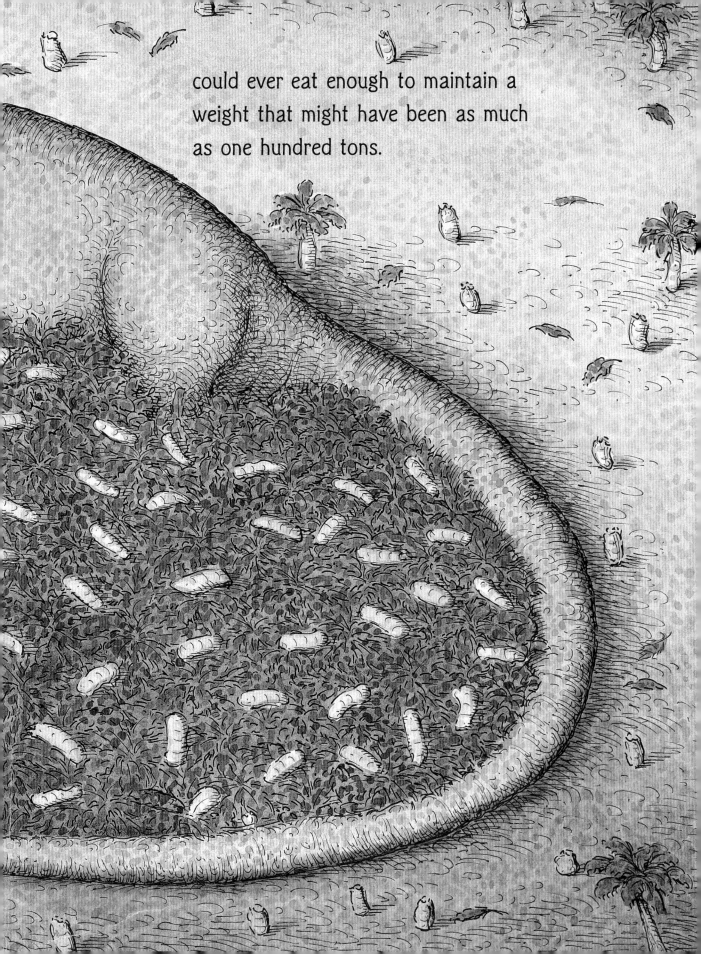

We may never know exactly how much a dinosaur weighed when it was alive, and different scientists can disagree by as much as twenty or thirty tons in estimating weights.

Tyrannosaurus rex may have been the largest
meat eater ever. But the jury is still out as to
whether T. rex mostly hunted for its food or mostly
scavenged to find dinner that was already dead.

Some paleontologists think Parasaurolophus
may have called out to other dinosaurs by
blowing or snorting through its hollow crest.

But unless somebody uncovers a 75-million-
year-old CD, we'll probably never know what
sounds dinosaurs made.

How dinosaurs courted and mated is full of mysteries. Perhaps male dinosaurs strutted their stuff to attract a mate, but in most cases it's

not possible to tell a male fossil from a female, let alone determine what a lady dinosaur might have looked for in a gent.

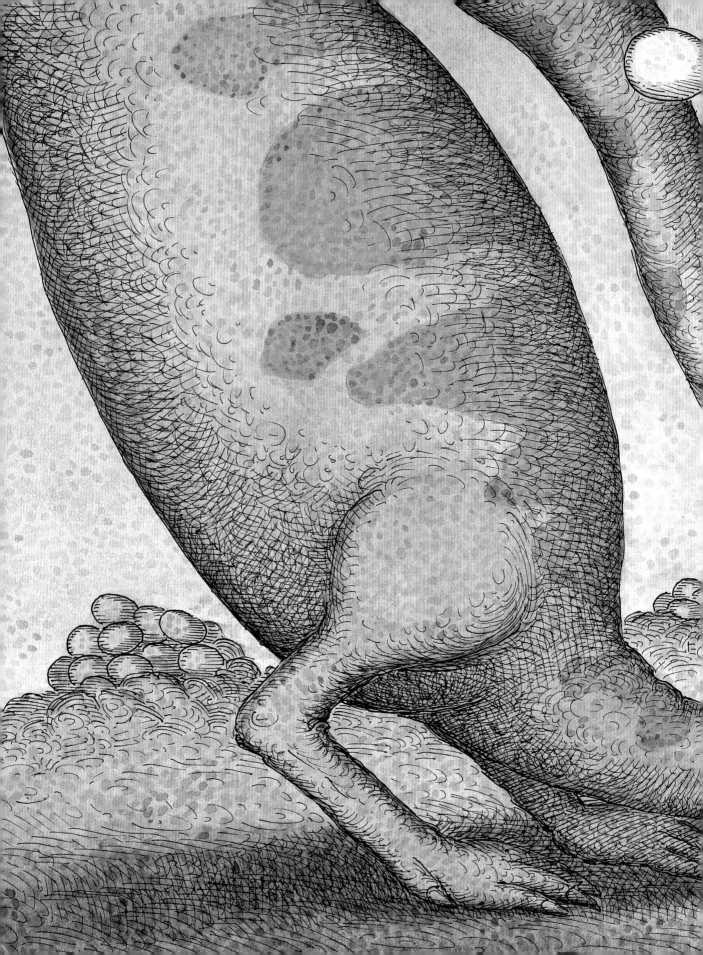

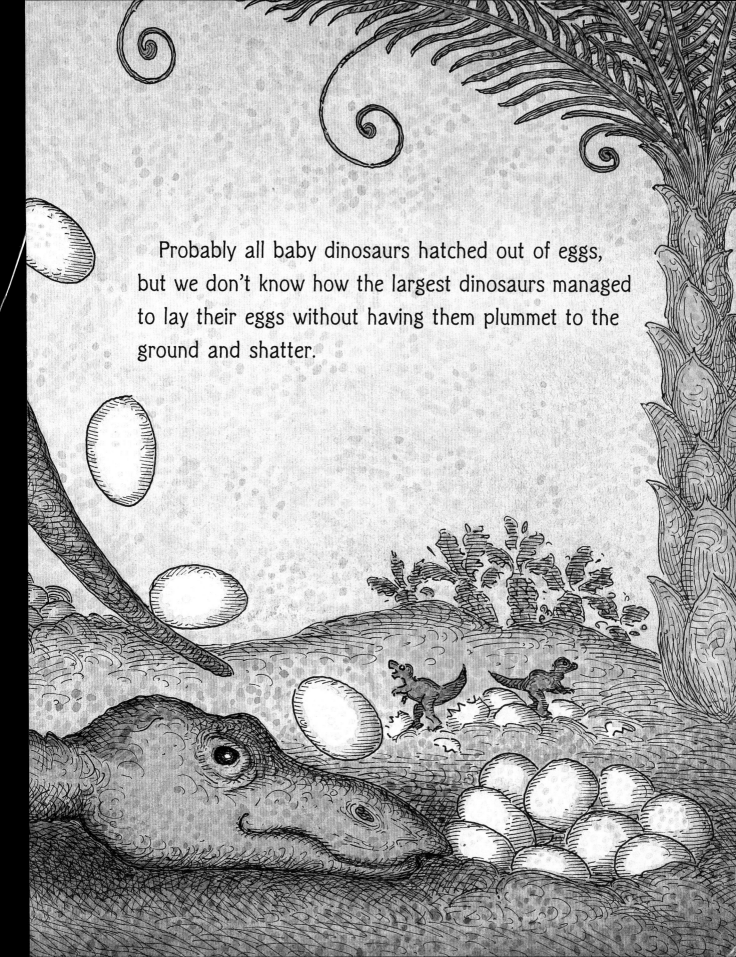

Probably all baby dinosaurs hatched out of eggs, but we don't know how the largest dinosaurs managed to lay their eggs without having them plummet to the ground and shatter.

Maiasaura got its name, which means "good mother lizard," from fossil evidence that Maiasaura parents took care of babies in their nests. Despite

the "good mother" label, we have no way of knowing whether it was the mothers, the fathers, or both, or even aunts or uncles who did the babysitting.

FIGURE 1

FIGURE 2

Spinosaurus had six-foot spines down its back, which probably supported an enormous sail or fin. Was the sail used to help Spinosaurus warm up and cool off, or was it used for protection or for attracting a mate? It's an unsolved mystery, and so are the back plates of Stegosaurus and the neck frill of Triceratops.

We don't know which dinosaurs came out by day and which ones, if any, came out by night or where they slept.

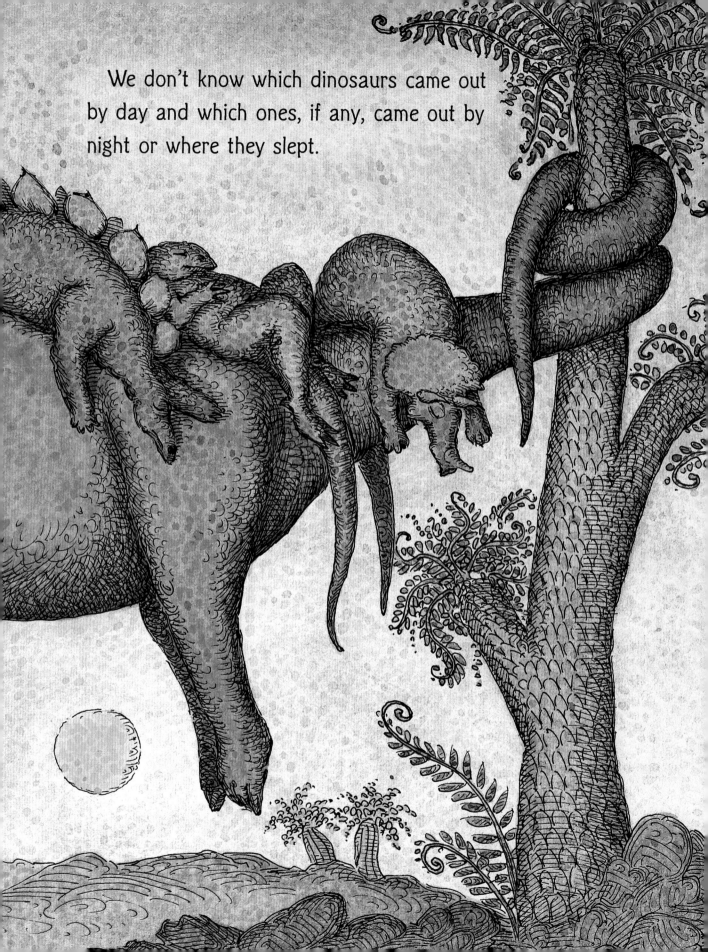

Experts disagree as to whether most dinosaurs
were cold-blooded, like their modern reptile cousins,
or warm-blooded, like the birds that may well be
living dinosaurs.

And while many scientists think that dinosaurs died out soon after a large asteroid or comet crashed into our planet about 65 million years ago, we still don't know for sure why they disappeared from the face of the earth.

There's a lot we don't know about dinosaurs, all right. But look at the bright side. How much would you want dinosaurs to know about you?

AUTHOR'S NOTE

Most scientists now agree that birds evolved from dinosaurs, and a convincing case can be made that, as long as birds survive, dinosaurs aren't really extinct. Since there is still some disagreement on whether birds should be considered dinosaurs, I have followed tradition in using the word *dinosaur* to refer only to extinct dinosaur species of the Mesozoic Era.